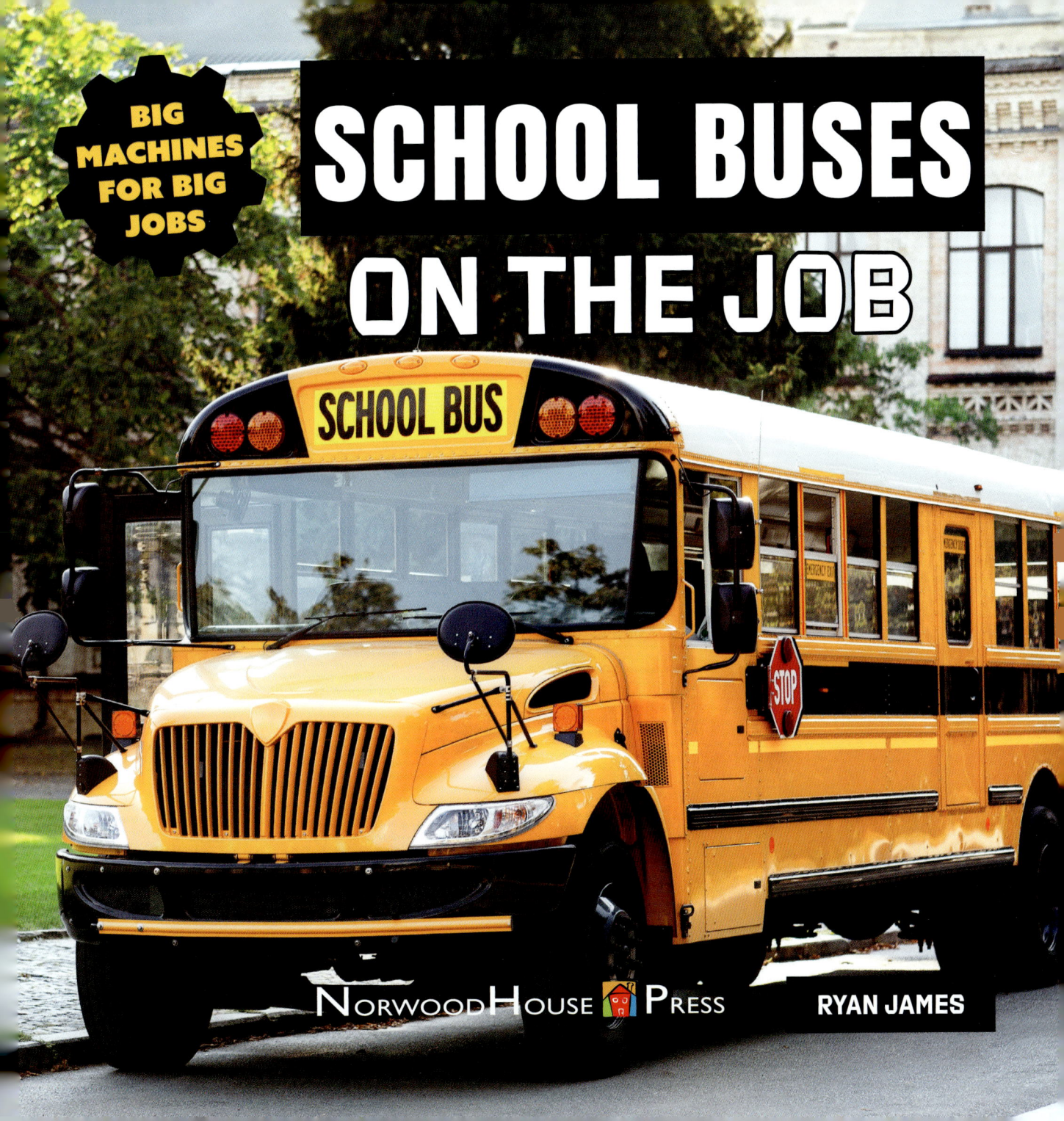

BIG MACHINES FOR BIG JOBS

SCHOOL BUSES
ON THE JOB

SCHOOL BUS

STOP

NORWOODHOUSE PRESS

RYAN JAMES

Cataloging-in-Publication Data

Names: James, Ryan.
Title: School buses on the job / Ryan James.
Description: Buffalo, NY : Norwood House Press, 2026. | Series: Big machines for big jobs | Includes glossary and index.
Identifiers: ISBN 9781978573932 (pbk.) | ISBN 9781978573949 (library bound) | ISBN 9781978573956 (ebook)
Subjects: LCSH: School buses--Juvenile literature.
Classification: LCC LB2864.J359 2026 | DDC 371.8'72--dc23

Published in 2026 by
Norwood House Press
2544 Clinton Street
Buffalo, NY 14224

Copyright © 2026 Norwood House Press
Designer: Rhea Magaro
Editor: Kim Thompson

Photo credits: Cover, pp. 1, 5, 6, 9, 18 Prostockstudio/Shutterstock.com; p. 3 SarahJaneJ/Shutterstock.com;p. 7 Pat Shrader/Shutterstock.com; p. 8 Andrew Angelov/Shutterstock.com; p. 10 Inside Creative House/Shutterstock.com; p. 11 Viktoriia Hnatiuk/Shutterstock.com; p. 12, 13 SnapshotPhotos/Shutterstock.com; p. 15 Ernest R. Prim/Shutterstock.com;p. 17 Dean Drobot/Shutterstock.com; p. 19 sonya etchison/Shutterstock.com; p. 21 Chepko Danil Vitalevich/Shutterstock.com;

Printed in the United States of America

Some of the images in this book illustrate individuals who are models. The depictions do not imply actual situations or events.

CPSIA compliance information: Batch #CSNHP26: For further information contact Norwood House Press at 1-800-237-9932.

Find us on

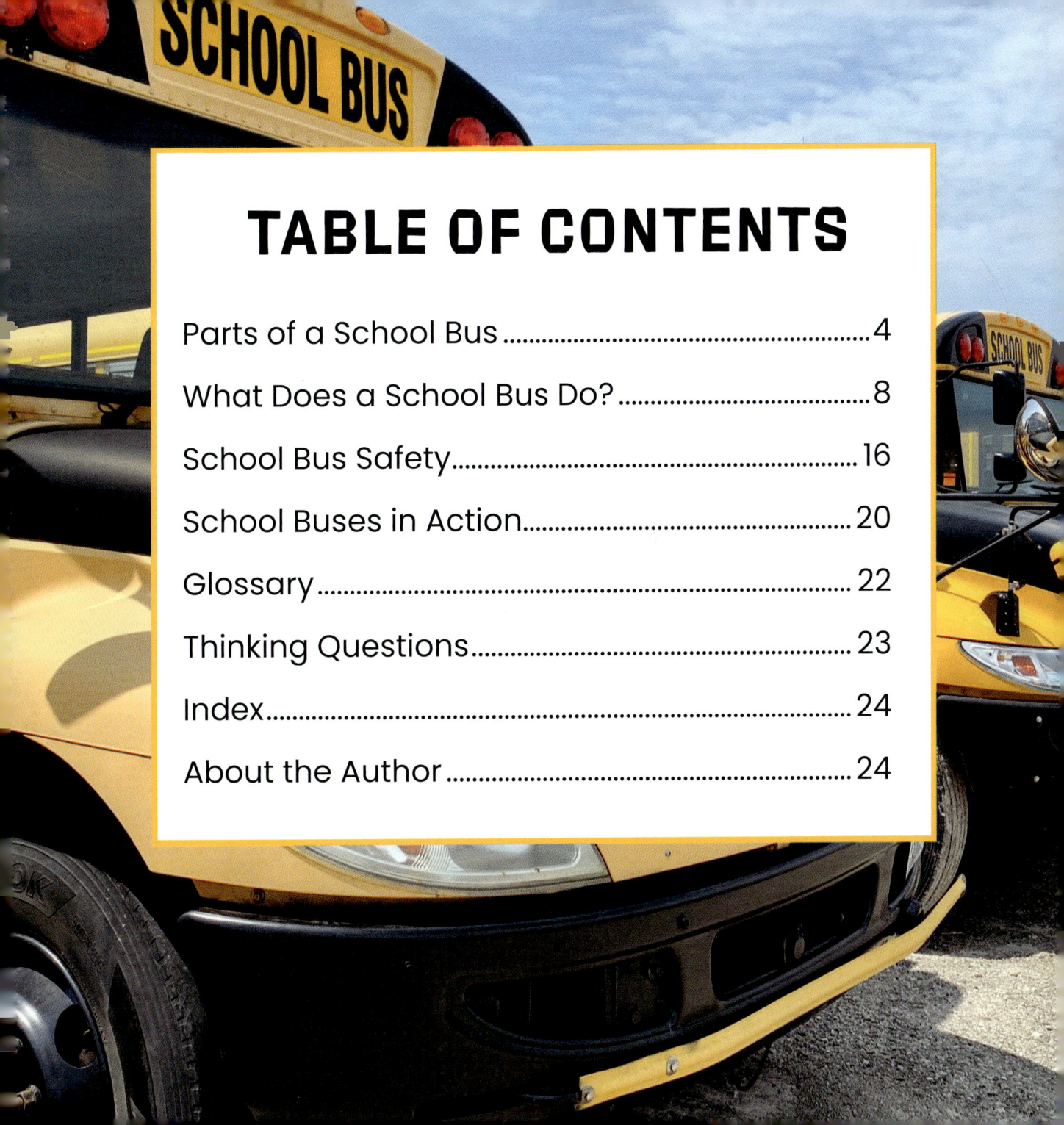

TABLE OF CONTENTS

PARTS OF A SCHOOL BUS

School buses are big **machines**. Most school buses have six wheels. All school buses have **flashing** lights.

The front of the bus has a seat for the driver.

There are windows on the sides.

There are rows of seats for students.

WHAT DOES A SCHOOL BUS DO?

School buses take students to school. They make sure students get home safely.

School buses drive for **field trips**.

They drive for after-school activities.

Students ride on the bus. They must stay seated. Some buses have seatbelts to keep students safe.

Students can look out the windows.

They can talk quietly to their friends.

Bus drivers follow a **route**. Each day, they go to the same neighborhoods.

13

Drivers stop to let students on and off. They turn on safety lights. This tells other drivers to stop.

SCHOOL BUS SAFETY

It is **important** to stay safe when you ride on a school bus.

Listen to the bus driver. Keep the **aisle** clear. Wait for the bus to stop before standing up.

When you walk near a school bus, make sure the driver can see you. Never walk behind a school bus.

Be **careful** when you walk in front of a school bus. Stay far out in front of the bus.

SCHOOL BUSES IN ACTION

School buses are **vehicles** on the job.

They keep students safe every day!

GLOSSARY

aisle (ile): the space between rows of seats; the middle of the bus

careful (KAIR-fuhl): paying close attention so that you stay safe

field trips (feeld trips): group trips to places where you can see things and learn about them

flashing (FLASH-ing): blinking on and off quickly

important (im-POR-tuhnt): needing your attention; key

machines (muh-SHEENZ): devices that do work

route (rout): the path a bus follows to pick up and drop off students

vehicles (VEE-i-kuhlz): machines used to move people or things from one place to another

THINKING QUESTIONS

1. What is the job of a school bus?

2. Name different parts of a school bus.

3. Why do school buses have lights that flash?

4. How can you stay safe around a school bus?

5. Why are school buses important?

INDEX

ABOUT THE AUTHOR

Ryan James lives in the mountains of North Carolina where he goes hiking with his dog Bailey. He loves fly fishing, visiting farms in the area, and picking fresh produce. He has always enjoyed writing and wrote his first book as a teenager.